XI'AN : Places of Historical Interest

張志勇　Jonny

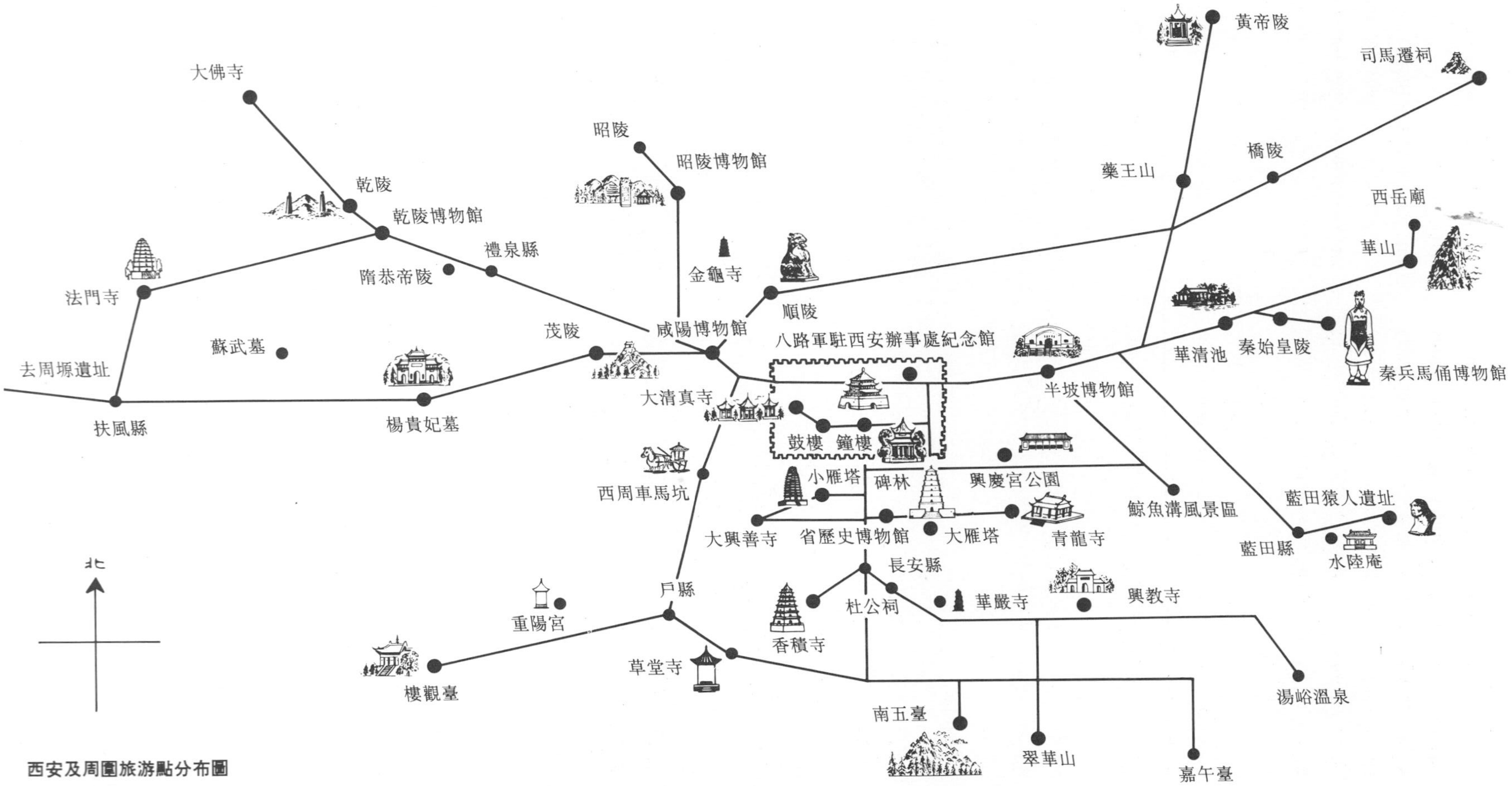

西安及周圍旅游點分布圖

陳敘新繪制

北

去周原遺址

法門寺

扶風縣

蘇武墓

大佛寺

乾陵

隋恭帝陵

乾陵博物館

楊貴妃墓

禮泉縣

昭陵

昭陵博物館

茂陵

咸陽博物館

金龜寺

重陽宮

西周車馬坑

大清真寺

順陵

八路軍駐西安辦事處紀念館

草堂寺

戶縣

大興善寺

省歷史博物館

小雁塔

鼓樓

鐘樓

碑林

香積寺

杜公祠

長安縣

大雁塔

興慶宮公園

青龍寺

半坡博物館

藥王山

華清池

秦始皇陵

橋陵

黃帝陵

司馬遷祠

樓觀臺

南五臺

翠華山

華嚴寺

興教寺

鯨魚溝風景區

藍田縣

藍田猿人遺址

水陸庵

華山

西岳廟

秦兵馬俑博物館

嘉午臺

湯峪溫泉

Hukou Falls

Survey of Xi'an (Chang'an)

Xi'an was known as Chang'an from the Han Dynasty to the Ming Dymasty (2 century. B. C. -14 century. A. D.) . Since the early Ming Dynasty it had been called xi'an.

Chang'an(Xi'an) was one of China's six ancient capitals, the other five Beijing, Luoyang, Kaifeng, Hangchow and Nanjing. Xi'an served as a capital for thirteen feudal dynasties including the Zhou, Qin, Han, Sui and Tang, for more than 1062 years. In the dynasties of Han and Tang, Chang'an was world famous for the start of the Silk Road. It was the political, economic and cultural center, and was also one of the largest and one of the most important cities in world history.

Xi'an (Chang' an) now the capital of Shaanxi Province, is situated in the middle of the Central Shaanxi Plains with beautiful landscape, fertile land and temperate climate. To its north lies the Wei River and Jing River, to its south stands Mt. Qinling, to its east run the Chan River and BaRiver, to its west the Feng

Bird's – eye View of Xi'an

River and the Lao River. The whole city covers an area of 9,983 m².

The Central Shaanxi Plain stretches from Tongguan to Baoji and is about 360km long from east to west. It is the major agricultural area for grain and cotton. Xi'an is situated in the middle part of this area. Mt. Qingling stands to the south of Xi'an, and serves as the natural dividing line between the north and the south of China. Xi'an annual average temperature is 13.3℃ and the annual average precipitation is 600mm. January is the coldest in the year when the average temperature is -6℃. July and August are the hottest, the average temperature is 29.7℃. The rainy season are three months –

– July, August and September, and the average precipitation is about 100mm. The main crops are wheat, rice, corn, cotton, sorghum, apple, walnut, pear, peach, apricot and water – melon.

Strolling about Xi'an is like being in a natural Chinese history museum, which houses a complete array of historical sites of different historical periods. We can see traces of the Tang Dynasty, which the streets were neat and in good order. As the famous poet of the Tang Dynasty Bai Juyi wrote: "streets are orderly arranged tike the neat vegetable plots." The Xi'an Forest of Stone Tablets known as "library of stone inscriptions," the site of matriarchal clan

2

community (Banpo Village), the time – telling Bell Tower and the Drum Tower of the Ming Dynasty, the magnificent city wall of the Ming Dynasty, the Big Wild Goose Pagoda and the Small Wild Goose Pagoda, the Great Mosque, in the rural areas the Mausoleum of Yellow Emperor, worshipped by the Chinese people as their ancestor located the north of Xi' an, and the world famous pottery center (Yao county), the Xingjiao Temple, the xing shan Temple, the qinglong Temple and the Caotang Temple south of Xi' an, Emperor Qin Shihuang' s Mausoleum and the Terra – Cotta Army known as the eighth wonder of the world and the Bea-

con Tower on Mauntain Li to the east, the site of buried carriges and horses(8B. C) of the West Zhou Dynasty and the site of Epang Palace of the Qin Dynasty, appeat to visitors all over world.

Since the establishment of the People' s Republic of China, Xi' an has become a modem industral and agricultural base.

Xi' an is attracting more and more tourists both at home and abroad with is unique resources, With the development of the travel industry, more and more attention will be paid to Xi' an by people all over the world.

The City Wall of Xi'an

The city wall stands in the central urban area of Xi'an. The length from east to west is a bit longer than that from south to north, in a shape of oblong. The perimeter is 11.9km. THere are four gate towers. The North Gate is named Anyuan Gate, the South Gage is Yongan Gate, the West Gate is Anding Gate and the East Gate is Changle Gate. The city wall was to rebuilt to a larger size on the site of the palace wall of the Tang Dynasty during Years 7 to 11

of Hongwu(1374 – 1378) in the Ming Dynasty. It has a history of 600 years, and it is one of the most largest, solid and complete ancient city walls still existing in China.

Over 1000 years ago, the Tang Dynasty set its capital on the present site of Xi'an. At that time the perimeter of the city wall of Chang'an was 35km. Such a huge structure was rare in world history, and Chang'an, Rome, Athens, Cario were known as the four biggest, ancient

capitals in the world. Chang' an fell into ruin after the war at the beginning of the 10th century. In the seventh year of Hong Wu of the Ming Dynasty (1374A. D.) Zhu Shuang made the city wall higher and wider on the base of the former one, forming the scale of the present city wall.

The city wall is 12m high the top is, 15m wide, the bottom is 18m, the battlement is 1. 65m high. There are brick water troughs for drainage. There is a gate tower and an arrow tower attached to the city wall in four directions. Three walls connecting the gate tower form four endosed places.

There is tower in front of the each enclosed place which one to operate the suspended bridge. The three towers match each other with the up – turned eaves high in the air. The structure is magnificent. A moat, wide and deep, runs around the city wall, so the whole city is strongly fortified.

South City Wall

The Banpo Village

The site of Banpo village is at Banpo cillage, 5 km on the eastern outskirtsts of Xi' an. It is a typical neolithic village of 6000 years ago. Found In the Spring of 1953, it was excavated five times on a big scale by the Chinese Academy of Sciences, the is 10, 000 m² which is one fifth of the site. The things That have been excavated are: 45 houses, 2 stables 6 kilns, more than 200 storage caves, more than 250 burial places for adulits as well as for children in pottery burial jars, more than 10, 000 pieces of tools and utensils, cores of fruits, bones of animals and rotten millet. In 1958 the Xi' an Banpo Museum was built. Besides the exhibit hall, over the site of the remains of 3000m² a protection hall was built. It is a historical site designated for state protection.

The site of the Banpo Village was divided into dwelling, pottery and burial areas. According to the archaeological research, it was a matriarchal clan community leading a life of a primitive communist society. In this primitive society. women were the main force and organizers in production, engaging in pottery, weaving, rasing domestic animals and farming, wiht men hunting, fishing and fighting.

Banpo village was in the loess area, so the soil was spongy. The production tools used by our ancestors include stone axes, knives, spades and hoes, as well as wooden tools such as digging sticks and hoes.

A completely preserved horizontal kiln was excacated here, which is one of the most ancient horizontal pottery kiln sites in China. There are about 60 kinds of utensils: cooking pots, tripods, tip – bottomed bottles, narrow – necked flasks, gourd – shaped pots and bowls. They were painted with various patterns, some were geometric patterns, some were fish with a big mouth, some were running deer and the design of a fish with a human face. Some were even with carced signs, They were characters of spells of they implied a deeper meaning. All these need further study and research.

The public adult grave yard of the community is in the northern part of the site, the burial way was different for adults and children. Some abults were buried with their faces up and

Bowl with the Pattem of A Fish and A Human Face

Tip – Bottomed Bottle

Stone Bracelets, Bone and Shell Ornaments

Stone Axe

limbs straight, and some with their faces down and limbs bended. The burial pits are arranged in good order with burial articles. Only adults were buried in public grave yard, children were buried near the dwelling placs, usually their corpses were in coarse jars. The famous archaeologist Guo Moro once wrote: " Children's corpses were buried in jars in Banpo Village, with a hole in the cover, letting the air in and out. The graves of children were beside the residence, just like lying in the bosoms of their mothers, the love and care for the young ones will never end. " These words point to the love and tender feeling of our ancestors for the younger generation.

Mausoleum of Emperor Qin Shi Huang

Emperor Qin shihuang's Mausoleum is located in Lintong County, 35km east of Xi'an. Mt Lishan is to the south of the mausoleum and Weihe river is to the north. The mausoleum is high up and overlooks the Central Plains. The huge size and the rich funerary objects make it unmatchable with all the mausoleums of the emperors in China.

Emperor Shihuang (259-210 B. C) alias Ying Zheng, came to the Qin throne at the age of 13, and took control of the state at the age of 22. By 221 B.C. he had annexed six rival principalities: the Han, Zhao, Yan, Wei, Chu and Qi, and established the first feudal empire in Chinese history. Ying Zheng created the

Position of emperor for himself and maintained this system. He ordered books of various schools to be burned and Confucian scholars to be buried; He adopted the perfecture and county system, and standardized legal codes, written language, axle length for carts, currencies and weights measures. All these measures played an important role in promoting and developing the economy and culture of the feudal dynasties of past ages.

In July, 210 B. C. Emperor Qin Shihuang died in Shaqiu(the present Julu County, Hebei Province,)on an inspection tour of the country. He died at the age of 50 after 37 yearsin reign. After Hu Hai the second son of Emperor Shihuang inherited the throne Emperor Qinshi-hang, Was buried at Lishan Mountain.

According to"Records of the Historian" by Sima Qiao, inside the tomb was a hall where a hundred seats were placed for high – rank officers. Buried inside were raer and valuable stones and jewellery. Rivers and lakes of mercury were constructed to symbolize the

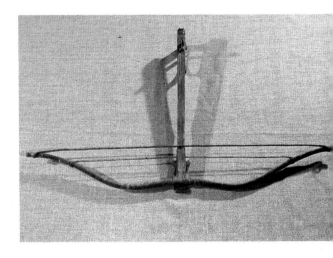

earth. The sun, the moon and stars of pearls and gems were made to symbolize the celestial body. Eternal lamps were lit with grease. The tomb was also protected by crossbows, which would discharge automatically if anyone tried to plunder the tomb. Emperor Epshi held a grand funeral for Emperor shi-huang, He cruelly ordered that all the palace maids who had not given birth to any children be sacrificed. To keep the secret of the mausoleum, the builders, who installed the internal arrows and arranged the treasures inside the tomb, were buried alive insied the mausoleum.

Emperor Qin Shihuang Conscripted more than 700, 000 convicts to build his mausoleum immediatelly after he came to the throne, and it cost 37 years. According to " Records of The Historian", the height of the mausoleum is 116m. Now it is 51, 668m high and the circumference is 2500m. The whole of cemetery is 15km in circumference.

The Weight of a Sliding Steelyard

9

Emperor Qin Shihuang's
Terra – Cotta Warriors & Horses

Emperor Qin Shihuang's Terra – Cotta Warriors and Horses are located 1500m east of the mausoleum. In march, 1974, Yang Zhifa and other five villagers discovered the pit while sinking a well.

This new discovery stirred up a sensation across the whole world. After several years of continuous excavation by the archaeologists, the Museum of Emperor Qin Shihuang's Terra-Cotta Warriors and Horese were constructed on the site of Pit No. 1 and was officially open to the public in October, 1979.

The museum occupies an area of 200,000 square meters, there are three pits named Pit No. 1, Pit No. 2, Pit No. 3 to the excavation. There are 7000 pottery figures in Pit

Excavation Site

Under Excavation

No. 1, including horses, chariots, infantry, cavalry. From their military robe we can see there are generals and soldiers of various military ranks. The average height of the terra – cotta figures is 1. 8m, but all some about 2. 1m. The terracotta figures in the three pits are arrayed in a practical battle formation with commanders facing east, as if they were ready to fight and conquer the six eastern states. The battle formation is an example for us to study the military strategy and tactics of 2, 000 years ago.

Thousands of real weapons were unearthed from the pits including swords, halberd spears, broad swords, battle – axes, crossbows, arrows and arrow heads. Some of the weapons were oxidated with chromate when made so they are still shining and sharp. Pit No. 1 is 5m deep, 230m long from east to west, 62m wide from noth to south and covers an area of 14, 260m². It is an attacking battle formation with foot soldiers and chariots.

Pit No. 1 is an earth – and – wood structure in the shape of a tunnel. There are five sloping entrances on the south and north side of the pit and five doors on the east and west side of the pit respectively. The terra – cotta warriors are of 38 column formation with for – hores drawn chariots among them. Pit No. 2 is located 20m to the north of the east end of Pit No. 1 and is

Pottery Horses and Figures

Arrow – heads

L – shaped pit. The pit is 5m deep, 124m long from east to west, and 98m from north to south, with an area of 12. 162m², There are 89 chariots with 356 horese, 116 horses for cavalry men and more than 900 various warriors. It is a battle formation of warrios with arrows and bows, cavalry men, infantry men and chariots. The system of arrangement is more complicated than that Pit NO. 1. Pit No. 3 is 5m deep, of concave shape covering an area less than 500m². The pit is divided into south, middle and north areas. In the middle area there is a chariot, there are guards of honour with weapons a long pole, standing in a cricle in the north and south areas, so it is most likely a command center though this has not been proved. The amazing and mysterious undergroung mighty army of 2, 000 years ago is attracting a continuous flow of visiters both home and abroad. Chirac, the exprime minister of France, exclaimed, " There are seven wonders in the world, the discovery of Qin Shihuang Terra – Cotta Warriors is the eighth wonder. " Thus the saying of "the world's eighth wonder" goes all over the world. No wonder the sophisticated politician exclaimed: "If you don't visit the Terra – Cotta Warriors, you can not say you have been to China. "

No. 1 Bronze Chariot

Bronze Chariots and Horses

In 1980, two sets of large painted bronze chariots and horses were unearthed. Probably they were intended for Emperor Qin Shihuang's soul to go out on inspection. They are the most big and most luxuriously ornamented bronze chariots and horses ever unearthed of in the world. The chariots and horses are exact imitations of the actual ones in half – life size. The function of every pary can work exactly like the real one.

They were listed as No. 1 and No. 2 according to their excavation. No. 1 Chariot was the leading chariot named"High Chariot". There is a copper umbrella over the chariot, and a sitting general with a copper sword his waist is driving it. There are crossbows and copper arrows in the front left trunk. NO. 2 Chariot was named " Security Chariot" and has a round cover above the square below. The chariot was made according to the concept of the na-

No. 2 Bronze Chariot

ture. The weight of the chariot is about 1. 8 tons. It is formed of more than 300 concept of the ancient people to nature parts like the No. 1 Chariot, and every part can function flexibly like a real one. The umbrella – like canopy on top is 4mm thick and the edge is only 1mm. There are windows on four sides and they can be opened at various angles, thereby controling the temperature and ventilation of the chariot. There are 30 spokes in the wheel. The chariot is luxuriouly decorated. There are more than a thousand pieces of gold and silver ornaments.

These chariots are the largest imitations the actual chariot ever unearthed. The skill of manufacturing is incomparable. The expansion joins used to make the wheels, which has only recently been adopted. But the ancestors were able to do it 2, 000 years ago. The powder wele process was used for many parts very skillfully. It remains a mystery as to how they coped with such complicated technology.

Emperor Liu Che & Maoling Mausoleum

Maoling, the mausoleum of the fifth Emperor Li Che (157 – 87B. C) of the Western Han Dynasty, is located about 40km west of Xi'an.

There were 11 emperors on the throne for a duration of 240 years nine of including Emperor Liu Che, were buried in the Xianyang Plateau along the north bank of Weihe River. The tombs streched about 40 km. The Western Han Dynasty typically built tombs on the plateau.

In the second year(139 B. C.) of his reign, the project of the Emperor's mausoleum was initiated, and it took 54 years to complete. According to historical records, the annual espenditure for building the tomb was one – third of the gross national product. Emperor Liu Che's burial objests were very extravagant. His burial objects were so many that the tomb could not hold them after his death due to the during the 53 years.

Liu Che was the emperor on the throne for the longest time in the Western Han Dynasty. His reign was the most prosperous and powerful so his mausoleum was the biggest and most sizable among the mausoleums during that period. In the 1930's, an American pilot, taking photos in the air, took Maoling Mausoleum for his discovery of a " pyramid" in Chian. The mausoleum was constructed in the shape of a forusideddipper, it is 46. 5m high, the perimeter of the bottom is 960m an area of 54, 540 m^2 meters According to the records of history, the tomb keepers, low – rank officials, cleaners and gardeners alone numbered more than 5000. The

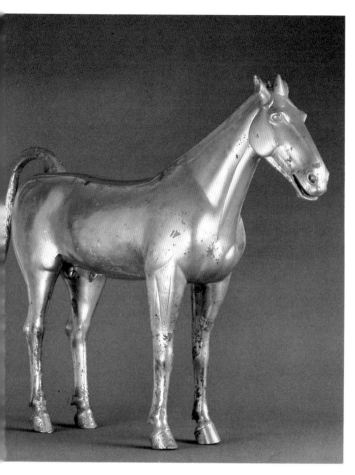

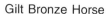
Gilt Bronze Horse

Eaves Tile with A Deer Pattem

high officials and noble lords who migrated to around the mausoleum numbered 270. 000. So it became the target of grave robbers in history. Nevertheless, there were still surprising relics unearthed recently, such as the remains of the construction, the utensils for daily life and production, the gilt bronze horse and the gilt silver fumigator. The manufacturing is unique and exquisite, and the art value is of international fame.

Emperor Liu Che was an excellent and talented politician and military strategist. During the 54 years of his reign, he launched battles to defeat the invaders on the northern borders and secured the peace there. He achieved success in politics conomys, science and culture. He established and promoted the relationship with other countries and opened the wellknow "Silk Road" to Middle – West Asia. He made great contributions to the development and progress of the world culture.

Huo Qubing's Tomb

Huo Qubing(140 – 117 B. C.) was an illegitimate child of Wei Shaoer, whose sister was Emperor Wudi's favourite concubine. He liked shooting with a bow. At the age of 18, he went with his uncle, General Wei Qing, to defeat the Hun invaders. He once defeated 2000 Hun invaders with his troop of 800 and got outstanding military exploit. Between the age of 18 to 24, he went on six punitive expeditions Hun invaders and won each battle, thus guaranteeing greater security on the northwestern frontier. He became a favourite of Emperor Wudi and was honoured a valiant general. He died suddenly of disease at the age of 24 at Mt. Qilian. Wudi was deeply grieved and ordered to escort Huo Qubing's coffin to Chang'

an, and burry him near Maoling Mousoleum. His tomb was constructed with earth and stone into the shape of a hill resembling the Qilian Mountain. Gigantic statues of stone men and animals were engraved and installed at the tomb site.

The natural shaped stone, after a few artistic cuts, became absolutely stone, after a few artistic cuts, became absolutely lifelike – – simple, natural, vigorous and powerful. The art pieces were the crystallization of the wisdom of the ancient labouring people, and they also reflected the mighty force of the most prosperous Western Han Dynasty. They have added an important chapter to the history of art in China.

Bronze Fumigator

Stone Carvings

19

Emperor Li Shimin and

Zhaoling Museum

Located in Liquan County about 75km northwest of Xi'an, Zhaoling is the mausoleum of Emperor Li Shimin. It was constructed against a mountain, and it is the most magnificent among the 18 tombs of the Tang Dynasty.

Emperor Li Shimin was the second son of the first Emperor Li Yuan. He was on the thorn for 23 years (627 – 649 A. D.). Li Shimin was an emperor of rare gift and bold strategy. He knew how to judge and make proper use of people. trusted people and make proper use of people, trusted people who once were against him, and provided wide opportunities for airing views and adopted useful ones. During his rule there was a famous peril of " Well – Managed

Zhenguan Reign, " an example for the rulers of the later ages.

Li Shimin paid great attention to friendly relationships with the minorities, thereby promoting cultural exchange and economic development. He adopted a good – neighbour policy. In 641, he married Privcess Wencheng to the ruler of Tufan(Tibet) to maintain the stability of thesouthwestern border areas, enabling people to recuperate and increase its population. So he created the world's strongest and most prosperous grand empire. Li Shimin's talent, strategy and wise policies not only consolidated the centralized state power but also laid a solid foundation for the cultural and development of the Tang Dynasty.

Emperor Li Shimin in the 10th year of Zhenguan (636 A. D.) began to construct his tomb at his wife's suggestion of being buried against mountain, and the construction lasted 13 years. Owing to the powerful and prosperous condition of the Tang Empire and the great achievements of Li Shimin, the most skillful artists in the state had been mobilized to join in the construction of the Zhaoling Mausoleum.

Accrding to historical records, there were quite a few huge structures and stone carvings above the ground at Zhaoling. At the foot of the hill, the Scarlet Bird Gate and the Sacrificial Hall were to the south, the Sacrificial Altar and the Sima Gate were to the north. There were 14 stone statues of minority chiefs inside the gate. There were also east and west broad corridors, inside the corridors lay the world – famous relief horses. The Zhaoling Mausoleum was very precipitous, for the convenience of construction, plank roads were built along the cliff, Upon the completion of the construction, the plank roads were torn down to secuer the safety of the mausoleum, so the stone palace would hang up on the mountain slope isolated from the outside world.

During the Five Dynasties, a warlord, Wen

Mural of a *Foreign Dancer*

Mural of a *Maid*

One of the Six Zhaoling Bas – relief Stone Horses

Tao broke into the Zhaoling tomb where he found that it was alomst the same as that of Chang' an city, splendid and spacious. Along both sides of the passage were the eastern and western rooms with stone beds. There were stone chests on them containing iron boxes with ancient books. He took those treasures, thus they Were scattered among the ordinary people.

To the south of the mausoleum there were tombs of lords, princesses, civil and military officids arranged in the shape of a fan. All together there were 167 tombs near the Zhaoling Mausoleun.

The Zhaoling Museum is located in the area of Li JI' sgraveyard, who was a favorite official with Emperor Li Shimin. There are exhibition rooms for stone tablets, carvings and paintings and some precious relics were unearthed recently. The inscriptions on the stone talblets were works of famous calligraphers Chu Suiling and Qyang Xun in the Tang Dynasty, and the gorgeous tri – coloured glazed pottery of the Tang Dynasty, and murals which are rare art treasures.

Tri – coloured Glazed Pottery Maid

Tri – Coloured Glazed Pottery Rider

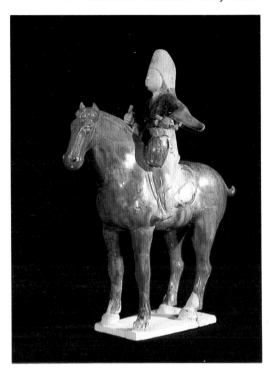

Pottery Figures from Zhaoling Museum

Emperor Tang Gaozong & Empress Wu Zeian's Mausoleum

Emperor Tang Gaozong and Empress Wu zetian's Qianling Mausoleum is located on Liangshan Hill in Qianxian County, 90km northwest of Xian. It is the only joint tomb of a marriedemperor and empress in Chinses hiseory. It is also one of the 18 mausoleums in the Tang Dynasty which, has been well preserved.

Emperor Tang Gan zong Named Li Zhi, the ninth son of Li Shimin, Emperor Tang Tai zong Li Zhi's mother was Empress Zhangsun who was strongly supported by her brother Prime Minister Zhangsun Wuji, ascended to the throne and was entitled Gaozong. He was on the throne

(650 – 683 A. D.)for 34 years. He died at the age of 56; in August of the following year, he was buried in Qianling Mausoleum. Wu Zetian (624 – 705 A. D.) was named Wu zhao. Her ancestral home was in Wenshui County in Shanxi Province. She was born in what is now Guangyuan County in Sichuan Province. Her father was the offcial in that area. Wu Zetian was a concubine of the fifth – grade concubine for emperor Tang Tai zhong. It is said that Li Shimin plannedto let her be buried alive with him after his death; She swore to become a nun stayed in the temple, and thus survived. Less

61 Headless Stone Statues

than a year after the death of Empreor Tai zhong, Empreor Gao zong let her return to the palace from Ganye Temple and very soon Wu zhe tian became the queen herself and replaced the former one. After the Emperor died in 684, she dethroned Emperor zhong zong and Empreor Reizong successively and set herself up as Empress, changed the name of the state to Zhou, gave the imperial title Wu, and became the only real empress in Chinese history. She was on the throne for 15 years. At the age of 82 she died in 705 A. D. in Xianju Hall of Shangyang Palace Luoyang. She was huried in 706 in Qianling in the Same grave with. Emperor Tang Taozong.

Chinese history has found Wu Zetian a controversial empress. Shrewd, pretty, and resolute, she gave full play to her ability to govern the country by helping Emperor Li Zhi (650 – 683 in reign) with national affairs, thereby worming into the emperor's favour. Her reign lasted 40 years and contributed much to the economic and cultural upsurge in the prine period of the Tang Dynasty. On her deathbed she agreed to change the title of the Dynasty from Zhou back into Tang (705). Meanwhile she raquired that a blank tablet be set up before her tomb, leaving her deeds open to comment. Few man can rival her in wisdom and magnanimity.

Liangshan Hill, a round and rocky one, is

Tomb of Prince Zhang Huai

1470m above sea level. Qianling Mausoleum is located on the north peak, occupying an area about 40km in circumference. To the south of the tomb are two peaks standing abreast and thus assuming the nickname of " Nipple Hills" . Seen afar, the three peaks appear much like a lady lying on her back. Exploation has proved that Qianling Mausloeum, of the 18 Tang tombs, is the only one that has almost untouched by premained grave robbers although it is very rich in treasure according to historical records. Rammed earth along the tomb passage remains the same as it used to. Built of Stone blocks, the tomb passage is 63m in length and 4m in width. of stone blocks are fastened together with iron bolts and all the crevices between the blocks are filled with molten lead. So solid is the construction that the tomb is to

Figures of an Officer and an Official

Tomb of Prince Yi De

make is to make defies any attempt of robbing Along the Heavenly Passage, which is 3km in length from south to north, stand statues of ornamental columns, winged horses, scarlet birds and human beings. Outside the north gate of the tomb are 61 stone statues of different sizes with a title inscribeb on the back of each statue. Researches show that they are heads of some minorities from the southwest of China. As distinguished guests, they attended the funeral of Emperor. To commemorate the event, Empress Wu ordered the stone statues carved.

Although the tomb has not been excavated for some technological reasons, the scene inside the tomb its appearance one day when tenchnology makes it possible to preserve the unearthed relics. Then the great works created by the Tang people will be a feast for the eyes.

winged Horse

Coloured Pottery Figurine

Mausoleum of Princess Yongtai

This is one of the 17 satellites to the Qianling Mausoleum. Li Xianhui, the tomb's occupant, was the seventh daughter of Emperor Li Xian (705 – 709in reign) as well as wife of Wu Yanji, who was a son of Wu Zetian's nephew. In 701, Wu Zetian had Li Xianhui and her husband secretly killed for their talk about her affairs with Zhang Yizhi and Zhang Zongchang. Dystocia was allegedly the cause of Li's death. Upon Wu Zetian's death, Emperor Li Xian was restored to the throne. The new Emperor conferred the title of Princess Yongtai upon his daughter and had her tomb, in 706, moved from luoyan to the present position, ironically serving as company to her grandparents.

Excavation of this tomb started in 1960. The tomb is composed of a passage about 87^5.

in length and 3.9m in width, five dorways, six sky – lights, an aisle lined with eight niches as well as two chambers. Very important are the mural paintings on the walls along the aisle. Although the tomb was once robbed, there remain 1300 pieces of exquisite funerary obiects including tri – colour glazed pottery figures, gold and silver ornaments, and jade articles. At the fifth sky – light is a skeleton and a hole, giving evidence of the robbery that happened sometime in the past.

The tomb has two chambers: the ante – cham – ber and the back chamber. The murals on the arched ceiling of the latter depict some celestial bodies, whereas those in the former are a vivid description of elegantly dressed maids with graceful carriage. They are typical of the fine arts 1300 years ago.

The Qianling Museum has been built at the exact site of Pricess Yongtai's Mausoleum. It houses numerous cultural relics mainly unearthed from the tomb of Prince Zhanghuai and the tomb of Prince Yide.

Maids of Honor with Oriental Beauty

Bottle, Bowl and Tray

Coloured Pottery Figurine

Shunling Mausoleum

This is where Wu Zetian's mother was entombed. Situated 40km to the north of Xi' an, the Shunling Tomb is under the jurisdiction of Xianyan and just by the expressway leading to Xi'anXianyang International Airport. According to historical records, Wu's mother died at the age of 92 in 670. Conferred the title of lady Jinguo, she was buried like an empress.

After Wu Zetian ascended to the throne in 689, she bestowed her mother a posthumous title of "Worthy Dowager." Her mother's tomb was expanded into the Shunling mausoleum. Though smaller in size than that of an emperor or prince, this tomb is famous of the stone carvings in front of it. Instances of the stone carvings include 13 statues of human figures, 3 stone sheep, a group of strolling, a group of unicorns, apir of squating lions and pair of ornamental pillars.

The strolling lions are 3.1m high and 3.4m long, striding proudly with a kingly bearing. The stone unicorns with a kingly bearing. The stone unicorns with wings are delicately created. It is believed that the unicorn's roar is powerful enough to bend every animal's will. Obviously both the lion and the unicorm are

Unicorn

placed here to guard the tomb.

The lion and the unicorn carved out of a single stone block, each with a weight of several tons. It is hard to imagine how the artists 1200 years ago moved and cared them into vivid statues. A highly artistic epitomization must have been employed in creating that master pieces.

Stone Lion

Huaqing Palace & Lady Yang

The Huaqing Palace, 30 kn east of Xi'an, is situated at the foot of Lishang Mountain, an extinct vocano about 1256m above sea leval. Seen afar, this mountain resembles a dark galloping horse which was called" Li" in ancient times. Therein lies the origin of the mountain's name. Construction of this palace dates back to the Western Zhou Dynasty (1100 – 771B). The palace was then intended for the emperor to take bath in the hot springs. The eighth century B. C. witnessed how king You fooled his generals or dukes by ordering the beacon tower lit when there was no invasion and how the Western Zhou perished. From then on the mountain has always been a reminder of that alarming

story in history. A tale It is also told that Qin Shi Huang (259 – 210B. C.) suffering traumas received some hints from a fairy maiden about a cure. To his surprise, the hints did help a lot. Therefore the hot spring won itselfa name for being favourable to one's health. Hot spring palaces have sice been built one after another in almost every dynasty. The culminating moment did not come until 747 when Emperor Li Longji (Xuanzong, 685 – 762) had an uprecedentedly resplendent palace built which housed the hot spring inside. It was named that Huaqing Palace. Because of on – and – off wars all the previous palaces fell into ruins. But thanks to the establishment of the People's Republic of

贵妃出浴图　　王海静 画

Origin of the Hot Spring

China (1949), a new palace has been erected on the base of a Qing Dynasty palace.

Lady Yang is one of the four beauties in Chinese history. It that all the flowers are too shy with her to come into bloom. What adds to the reputation of Huaqing Palace is the fact that Lady Yang, Emperor Li Longji's favourite, was granted the privilege of taking baths in the palace. Lady Yang, originally named Yuhuan, was born in Shuzhou Dresentday Sichuan Province. At 18 she became a concubine to Li Mao, one son of Emperor Li Longji. She was later favoured by the Emperor on Gao Lishi's

recommendation. To justify the relationship between Yang Yuhuan and the Emperor himself, Li Longji incited her to convert to Taoism and take Taizhen as her religious name. Before long she was wummoned back as a concubine to the Emperor rather than his son. Exclusive favour had been bestowed on Lady Yang ever since. Untold wealth and honour, as a result, were heaped upon the members of her family. Her cousin, Yang Huozhong was appointed to be the first Minister of the Empire; her sisters were also conferred distinguished titles. The four sisters were so appealing to the Emperor that his mind seldom dwelled on the business of the country. Instead, the emperor spared no effort to ingratiate himself with the beauties. A great rebelling led by two generals ensued, marking the decline of the Tang Empire.

Now at the sites of the Lily Pool, the Crabapple Pool, and alike, the Museum of the Tang Imperial Pools has been constructed and opened to visitors.

Modern Chinese history witnessed the Xi'an Incident is December 12, 1936, which shocked the world. The incident started, By Hucheng General Zhang Xueliang and General Yang Hucherg took place in the Huaqing Pool, paving path the for the second cooperation between the Communists and the Nationalists. To commemorate the event, the Remonstration Pavillion was built where Chiang Kaishek hid himself from the two generals' soldiers.

Lady Yang's Bathing Pool

Site of the Bathing Pools For Lady Yang and the Tang Emperor

Xingqing Palace

The Xingqing Palace, situated 1km to the southeast of the city, used to be the residence of Emperor Li Longji (685 – 762) and his four brothers. The present palace was built on the site of the Tang Palace in 1958. The Xingqing Palace of the Tang Dynasty evolved from Li Longji's residence. In 728, it became the political cantre of the country because Emperor Li

Longji started conducting state affairs here. Thanks to successive enlargements, the palace developed into an imperial park.

Among the great structrues inside the park are the Administrative Palace, the Fraternity Palace and the Agalloch Pavillion. The Administrative Palave was intended for the emperor to devote himself to state affairs. Ironically, the

Agalloch Pavilion

emperor was completely infatuated with lady Yang, as has been believed one of the main causes for An – Shi Rebellion (755 – 763). The Agalloch Pavillion is wurrounded by peonies which send forth a fragrance touching the traveller's heart. It was the right place for Emperor Li Linji and Lady Yang to appreciate to flowers. The love story between them gave inspiration to many men of letters.

The former exclusive imperial park now has been built into a recreational park open to the pubilc.

Monument to Abenonakamaro

Made of white marble, Monument to Abenonakamaro stands in the northeast of the Xingqing Park. It is 3. 6m high in the form of a pillar and in the architectural style of the Tang Dynasty （618－907） . On the farcade(facing north) is the inscription. " Monument to Abenonakamaro. " Inscribed on the east side is a poem by Abenonakamaro, missing his home town while on the west is a poem by Li Bai, mouring Abenonakamaro's death.

With Chao Heng as his Chinese name, Abenomakamaro was born in 698 in Nara, Japan. At the age of nineteen, he came to China as a Japanese envoy to the Tang Dynasty. He was active in the political arena. It is he who persuaded Jianzhen, a famous monk, to travel east to Japan to preach Buddhism. Upon his death in 770, he was posthumously conferred the title of " Great Marshal of Luozhou. "

The monument was erected on July 1, 1979 to observe the fifth anniversary of the reestablished friendship between Xi' an and Nara. The mounment, also a memorial of the Sino－Japanese friendship, has received numerous visitors from home and abroad. Now it has been listed as one of the historic monuments in Shaanxi Province.

Tomb of Lady Yang

The Tomb of Lady yang is situated in Mawei Village, Xingping County, about 70km away from Xi'an. Lady Yang (718 – 756), originally named Yang Yuhuan, was first a concubine to an emperor's son. Later the Tang Emperor Li Longji (685 – 762) found her desirable and took her as a consort. From then onwards, the Empoeror was completely infatuated with her and neglected his duties.

In 755, a rebellion was staged by An Lushan, Whose forces swiftly struck into the capital of Chang'an. Accompanied by a small group of relatives and courtiers, the Emperor fled south to Sichuan Province. Upon their arrival at Mawei Village, the soldiers mutinied and forced the Emperor to have Lady yang killed because they enraged with the members of the Yang family, believed the Yang falmily were responsible for the debacle. To survive, the Emperor ordered both Lady Yang and her cousin Yang Guozong dispatched. The burial wound rp hastily.

The tomb used to be an earthen mound about 3m in herght. Then why is it covered with bricks now? A tale has it that the earth of her tomb could preserve youthful looks because lady Yang is one of the four notorious beauties in Chinese history. Women nearby, therefore, would take a handful of the earth on lunar 3th. March every year when they passed by the tomb, trying to beautify themselves by applying it to their faces. by and by the tomb dwindled in size. Healing up could not keep up with dwindling. To protect it from constant shrinking, the local people resorted to bricks. That is how the tomb took its present shape. The story about lady Yang has so far – reaching an influence that it has been the subject of many poems and hramas.

Famen Buddhist Temple Prior to Renovations

Famen Buddhist Temple Museum

Famen Buddhist Temple

Famen Buddhist Temple, located 15km north of Fufeng County and 130km west of Xi'an began construction 147 of the Eastern Han Dynasty (25 – 220). It is among the most ancient temples in China.

It is believed that Asoka, King of India, divided the remains of Sakyamuni into 48, 000 portions, which were taken to various places of the world. China has 19 stupas that enshine such portions.

Famen Buddhist Temple Pagoda was a four – storeyed wooden structure when is was constructed. Later in the Ming Dynasty (1368 – 1644), Pagoda was added to 13 floors

to reach a height of 54m. In the Qing Dynasty (1616 – 1911). the pagoda cracked in the middle an earthquake and leaned a little to southwest consequently. To make things even worse, continuous rain resulted in the sudden collapse of half the pagoda on August 24, 1981. January of 1987 repairs began on the damaged pagoda and on April 3 (birthday of Sakyamuni) of the same year, the crypt was coincidentally discoveredwhen the foundation of the padoda was being cleared up.

The crypt houses four portions of Sakyamuni's finger bone and other valuable relics. The portion discovered first is placed in a tiny

41

Eight Gem – framed Serial Caskets

Mat Used When Buddha Is Worshipped

stupa of pure gold cased by eight gemframed gold and silver caskets in orderof size. The largest exterior casket the rest bears a of god guardian carved on each of four sides. What was discovered next is kept in a pretty stupa of marble in the central room of the crypt. The third discovery was put in a bemframed casket cased is a little niche at the rear room of the crypt. The fourth and last portion is in the bone stupa carved with Buddhas in colour paints at the front room of the crypt. Only one portion has been proved to be taken from the genuine finger bone remains of the Buddhism master. Although the other three are imitations, they are accepted in Buddhist circles with the same holy significance.

As was recorded on the tablet in the crypt, the finger bone remains of Sakyamuni were retained in the crypt of the temple from the Northern Wei Dynasty (386 – 534) down to the Sui Dynasty (581 – 618). Emperors of the Tang Dynasty (618 – 907) humbly brought the finger bone remains of the Buddha to the imperial palace five times for consecration. In 873, Emperor Li Xuan (Xizong, reigned 873 – 888) sent them back to the temple in the company of many imperial objects. From then on they remained hidden until discovered.

Censer

The imperial objects with gold and silver wares of the Tang Dynasty unearthed in the crypt not only abound in number, but also grade highly in quality. Silk fabrics were well preserved when unearthed. They provide powerful of the development in politics, culture and art of the Tang Dynasty.

Lastly, the discovered porcelain painted in a colour between blue and green made the first appearance before the world. So the 13 pieces of the kind unearthed from the crypt to the temple are the most fruitful findings in the archaeololgy of China wares The colour was used only in palaces and the preparation was kept secret to the outside.

Great Xingshan Temple:

Home of Vajrayana

The Great Xingshan Temple, 3km south of the city, is the one of the oldest tremendous temples. The temple has been proved to have a history of over 1700 years, It was first built sometime between 265 and 289.

Having been introduced into China, Buddhism reached its heyday in the Sui and Tang Dynasties Indian (581 – 907). It then that some devout Indian monks of great sanctity came to

China. Vajrayana underwent an unprecedentna and advocated the doctrine known as Mizong Buddhism. Meanwhile they rendered 278 volumes of Buddhist scriptures from Sanskrit into Chinese. The popularity of vajrayana was greatly promoted during the reign of Emperor Li Longji(712 – 756) by three Indian monks, one of whom is Amoghavajra. Wherever the Buddhist doctrine was preached, there would be

over ten thousanded development when the temple was in the charge of Amoghaveajra, who translated more than 500 volumes of the sacred scriptures. Hence the temple has been regarded as the fountainbead of Vajrayana.

In 845, Buddhism suffered a setback because Taoism was venerated instead. Great damage befell the temple. The temple didn't come into the present magnificent shape until 1955 when large – scale renovations were made. In one of the four yards at the temple stands an eyecatching and peace – blessing bronze Buddha presented by some Japanese Vajrayanists in 1986. Now the temple is the headquarters of both the Provincial Buddhist Association and the Municiple Buddhist Association.

Opening the Light

Caotang Temple

This temple made its first appearance in 401 during the Eastern Jin Dynasty (317 – 420). Due to an emperor's liking for Buddhism, a devout Indian monk named Kumarajive was invited to Chang'an and honoured as Great Master. The Caotang Temple, then named Xiaoyao Garden, was intended for him to deliver lectures on the Buddhist doctrine.

Having settled in the temple located at the foot of Guifeng Peak about 30km southeast of Xi'an Kumarajive translated 97 items in 427 chapters of Buddhist scriptures with the assistance of his 3000 followers. For this reason he has been regarded as the foreunner of translation from foreign languages into Chinese. Upon his demise, he was buried at the temple.

Well – perserved in the temple is a three – storeyed, octagonal dagoba of exquiste workmanship. 2. 33m in height, it really deserves the beautiful name, " The Eight – jaded Dagoda. "

More appealing is the So – called" Mist Well" in the bamboo grove at the backyard. Every moring there will be gusts of mist ascending out of the well, constituting a mysterious scene known as " the Mist of Caotang Temple. "

Statue of Kumarajiva

Stupa in Memory of Kumarajiva

Big Wild Goose Pagoda & Ci'en Temple

The Big Wild Goose Pagoda is located inb the Ci'en Temple about 4km south of the city. It is recorded that the temple was built on 648 when Li Zhi, then the Crown Li Zhi(650 – 683 in reign), then the Crown Prince, decided to have it set up to commemorate his mother. At that time the temple was of tremendous size, including over ten yards and thousands of rooms.

The construction of the pagoda owes much to agreat Buddhist monk religiously named Xuanzang and secularly called Chenyi. He was the founder of Faxiang Sect of Buddhism. In 629 during the reign of Li Shimin (599 – 649), he went on apilgrimage to India to perfect his knowledge of Buddhist philosophy. After an absence of 16 yearsm, he came back with 657 items of Buddhist Sauta, of which he translated 75 items in 1335 chapters. He ranks No. 1 as among the four great translators of Buddhist Scripture because his version is the largest in number, best in quality , and greatest in influence. In praice of his contribution to Buddhism, Emperor Li Longji composed An Introduction to the Sacred Teachings of Monk Tripitaka of the Great Tang Dynasty, which was later inscribed after the caligraphy of Chu, a famous calligraphy in the Tang Dynasty.

It is beyond doubt that the talbet with such inscriptions is a rare feast for the eyes. During the reign of Emper Tang Gaozong a special hall was built for Xuanzang to translate the sacred the sacred scriptures. To store the scriptures he had brought back India, Xuanzang made a proposal that a pagoda be constructed in imitation of an Indian one. Originally the pagoda was a five – storeyed brick structure. The renovation it 701 made it into a ten – storeyed one, whose top could be reached through the stairs installed inside. For some unknown reason, the pagoda changed into a seven –

Statue of Buddha

Scriptures Translated by Xuanzang

storeyed structure. Although it has been renovated from time to time, the pagoda remains a
seven – storeyed one. Despite dozens of earthquakes above magnitued 7 in the central plain
of Shaanxi Province after the Tang Dynasty, the
Big Wild Goose Pagoda stands lofty and firm,
giving ready evidence of the ancient people's
wisdom and talent in architecture.

Tablet with *An Introduction to the Sacred Teachings of Monk
Tripitaka of the Great Tang Dynasty*

Xingjiao Temple

The Xingjiao Temple, about 30km south of Xi'an, is situated on the Shaoling Hillock, facing Zhongnan Mountain across a small valley. It is now under the jurisdiction of Chang'an county.

Upon Master XuanZang's death at 56 in 664, he was first buried on the Bailu Hillock to the southeast of Xi'an. To commemorate the great master, Emperor Li Zhi (650 – 683 in reign), who was deeply grieved, had a stupq built to enshrine the master's remains. In 670 the Xingjiao Temple was completed just beside the stupa. Inscribed on the stuqa are two characters" Xingjiao" written by Emperor Li Heng (756 – 762 in reign). "Xingjiao" means "promothing Buddhism" in Chinese. Henceforth, it has been known as "Xingjiao Temple."

The temple faces south. Inside the front gate are two solemn structures by the main path: the bell tower and the drum tower. The main compound is winged with two yards where ancient cypresses grow luxuriantly. In the east yard stands the structure to shelter the Buddhist scriptures; in the west yard are three stupas, the middle one for Xuanzang and the other two for two of his disciples respectively named Kuiji and Yuance.

Facing Zhongnan Mountain and enjoying a fine location, the Xingjiao Temple is a feast for the eyes.

Dagobas of Xuanzang and his two Disciples

Buddha Statues

Altar Table

Xuanzang: Master of the Tripitaka

Xuanzang, honorary epithet Master of the Tripitaka, was namd Chenyi. Bom into a cultured family in 600, he had three brothers. At the age of 13, he entered Buddhist or ders. He went to Chang'an with his elder brother after he was initiated into monkhood at the age of 22. He spent the next few years visiting famous temples and studying Buddhist philosophy. Troubled by numerous discerpancies and contradictions in the tests he was reading, he decided to study at the fountainhead of Buddhism to perfect his knowledge of its doctrine. His request was not permitted. He set off by stealth at the age of 28. He made a perilous trip through the mountains and deserts of central Asia. At last he arrived in India.

Xuanzang stayed in the holy land of Buddhism, visiting all the sacred sites and studying all the sacred scriptures available. Despite the fact that Buddhism was at a low tide, Xuanzang made an intrepid and dfficient study of it. At Nalanda monastery, The greatest temple in India, he achieved an incredible victory in a debate. It is incredible because he argued for Mahayana instead of Hinayana, which dominated Buddhist philosphy at that time. His victory in the dedate established his eminence and reputatutation among Indian monks and other believers.

After an absence of 16 years, Xuanzang returned with a great number of Buddhist sutra. His reputation was so wide – spread as to reach many countries, including his motherland. Therefore he was accorded a tumultuous welcome at the capital of Chang' an. Much to his honour, he was recrived in audience by Emperor Li Shimin (599 – 649) and other offcials, who all had travelled 25km to meet him. Seldom in history was there an occasion in which an emperor would walk hand in hand with a monk as Li Shimin did.

Xuanzang translated the Buddhist scriptures at such temples as the Hongfu Temple, the Ci' en Temple and the Yuhua Temple. His translations totaled 75 items in 1335 chapters. Strenuous work impaired his health and claimed his life eventually. Though he died in 664, he left behind not only his translations but also a book titled Records of the Western Regions of the Great Tang Dynasty. This book is of inestimable value to historians and archaeologists.

Small Wild Goose Pagoda & Jianfu Temple

The Small Wild Goose Pagoda stands in the Jianfu Temple which used to be the residence of Princess Xiangcheng, a daughter of Emperor Li Shimin(599 – 649) . In 684, the Tang Emperor Li Dan ordered the residence reconstruched into a temple to observe the 100th day of his father' s death. The temple was named"Great Xianfu, " meaning in Chinese " offering happiness. " But Six years later when Wu Zetian dethroned her son and ascended the throne herself, she replaced the name with" Jianfu Temple", hence the present name. The temple is only 1. 5km south of the city wall.

The present temple was shaped by wars towards the end of the Tang Dynasty (618 – 907) and by renovations and removes in almost every dynasty.

The pagoda built in 709 was originally named after the temple. It was a 15 – storeyed brick structure with layers of eaves. Tall and graceful, the pagoda bore similarith to the Big Wild Goose Pagoda in architecture and height, so it came to be called the Small Wild Goose Pagoda.

According to a tombstone from the Ming Dynasty (1368 – 1644), an earthquake occurred in Xi' an in 1487, Leaving the pagoda split into halves with a rift as wide as one third metre. It is also recorded that 1520 witnessed another earthquake in the central plain of Shaanxi Province. Miraculously, the crack caused by the last quake closed up. No one could tell whether there existed a supernatural cause. but a folktale has it that an immortal deeply regretted the crevice in the sacred pagoda and the halves united again just by waving his whip as if rounding up sheep.

It is perfectly true that a crevice caused by earthquake can been seen in the pagoda. As a

Baiyi Pavilion

precaution against earthquakes, iron hoops have been bound around the pagoda. Besides, the Xi' an municipal government has installed the pagoda with some lightning devices. Inside the temple remains an iron bell made in 1192. During the Qing Dynasty (1644 – 1911), the monks tolled the bell on a daily dasis whose pleasant sound could be heard from afar. Gradually the sound of the bell from this temple became so reputable that the temple was listed as one of the eight scenis spots in Chang' an. The present pagoda in a 13 – storeyed structure at a height of 43m. The top two storeys were shaken off by another great earthquake that occurred in 1555 during the reign of Emperor Zhu Houcong (1522 – 1567) of the Ming Dynasty.

Xiangji Buddhist Temple

Statue of the Master

Xiangji Buddhist Temple, situated at the foot of Shenhe Hillock of Chang'an County and 17km southwest of Xi'an is regarded as the home of Jingth Sect of Buddhism (meaning land of purity).

The temple was built in 706 of the Tang Dynasty (618 – 907) to commemorate Master Shan Dao, founder of the sect. It has in it a stupa that houses the remained of the master. The stupa now has 10 floors left after two earthquakes in central Shaanxi, which shook off 3 floors from the top down.

Master Shan Dao was born at Linzi of Shandong Province in 613 and died in 681. After he moved to Chang' an County, he worked at Buddhist doctrines and set up a nes sect of Buddhism (Jin Tu school). His Buddhism works were introduced into Japan in the 8 th century, in the light of which a Japanese monk developed a similar sect which became widespread and influential across Japan. The Japanese dixciples worshipped Master Shan Dao as the patriarch. Naturally, Xiangji Buddhist Temple is the ancestral temple in their eyes.

Along with the restoration of relations between China and Japai, Japanese friends from various circles as well as Japanese disciples of the sect have been to the temple and the stupa many times. In 1980 when the 1300 th anniversary was marked to commemorate the death of the master, the stupa was renovated. The Precious Hall of the temple together with the affiliated chambers were re – built to take on new looks.

Great Hall in Memory of Huiguo and Kukai

Qinglong Temple & Master Hongfa

Built during the Dynasty (581 – 618), the Qinglong Temple was originally named Linggan Temple and adopted the present name in 711 during the Tang Dynasth (618 – 907). Close to the newly – built beltway around Xi' an, the temple is located only 4km southeast of the city.

In the Tang Dynasty, the Qinglong Temple was one of the greatest monasteries. When Huiguo, a disciple of a famous Indian monk known as Amoghavajre, started managing the temple, he initiated Zhenyan School, a sect of Buddhism.

Among the Japanese envoys to the Tang Dynasty in 804 was a monk with the name Kongkai, later known as Master Hongfa. Upon his arrival at the Qinglong Temple, he began to study under Huiguo, majoring in Vajrayana. As a matter of fact, his studies ranged over such fields as Buddhism, Taoism, medicine, music and culiary arts. When kongkai returned to Japan, he set up Zhenyan School in Japan. Accordingly he was honourd as the patriarch of Orient Vajrayana. For this reason. the Qinglong Temple has ever since been the fountainhead of that school in Japan.

The period from 658 to 849 witnessed 19 groups of Japanese envoys to the Tang Dynasty. Among these envoys, there were eight eminant and accomplished Buddhist masters, six of whom once studied Vajrayana at the Qinglong Temple. The most outstanding one is Kongkai who made indelible contributions to both the SinoJapanese cultural exchange and the development of Buddhism in Japan.

Unfortunately, the Qinglong Temple was utterly ruined by war after the Tang Dynasty. In 1982, some believers of the Zhenyan Buddhism in Japan, with the assistance of the Municiple Buddhist Association and the Municiple Government of Xi' an, set up a monument in memory of Kukai at the site of the former Qinglong Temple. Before long a hall came into existence nearby. to commemorate Huiguo and Kukai' s great contribution to Sino – Japanese friendship.

Unadorned and elegant, the temple bears great similarity to the Tang temple in architectual style. The compound is sprinkled with oriental cherries. In early spring, sweet fragrane permeats the temple, seemingly displacing all worries and cares from the visitors' minds.

Kong Hai Monument

Greater Mosque of Xi'an

The Greater Mosque of Xi' an lies at Huajuexiang Street northwest of the Drum Tower.

As revealed by what is written on the tablet in the mosque, the structures were built in the Tang Dynasty (618 – 907). Extensive repairs in the Ming Dynasty (1368 – 1644) finally made them in architectural style of the dynasty.

The mosque takes up a floor space of 12, 000m². It is comprises of four sizable yards. The major building in the front yard is an eight-meter high wooden memorial archway topped by glazed tiles with eaves turning up a little on at the edges. The stone tablets in the second yard record the repair work done in the Dynasties of Ming and Qing (1616 – 1911). The Month Tablet that stands west in the yard

was cared in Arabic and serves as a bevice to figure out time on the Moslem calendar. In the centre of the third yard stands a three storeyed octagonal structure, where Chinses Moslems assemble before paryer. Main buildings cluster in the fourth yard, which contains a compound structure of three connected hexagonal pavilions with eaves turning up a little the edges. The architecture is named Phoenix Pavilion. From there up are the corridor, the prayer hall and the main hall that accommodate over 1, 000 Moslems to say their parayers.

Every yard in the mosque is boasts its own features. Now, the mosque is open the the public, not only for Moslems, but also for distinguished guests from Arab countries.

Wooden Archway of the Greater Mosque

Phoenix Pavilion

China Islam

Islam is believed to have been introduced into China is 651 of the Tang Dynasty (618 – 907).

Historical documents reveal that Islam worked is way into China by two routes. The first route established for commercial trade was the Silk Road by land from west Asia to Chang' an through Mt Tianshan Xinjiang Uygur Autonomous Region, extended eastward later along the Yellow River. The other route established a little later the Sing Dynasty (960 – 1279) was by sea from the Indian Ocean to coastal areas of China's southeast and farther to the Hinterland.

Along with the development of commercial trade and the estblishment of diplomatic relations, Moslems from Arab countries began to settle down permanently in groups at Chang'an and coastal cities. More became settlers in the Yuan Dynasty (1206 – 1368).

As their beliefs and customs differ from those of the Chinese, the people of a new nationality in China, the hui. Through years of national interflow, they developed their own independent system of religious doctrine based mainly on Islam in the Qing Dynasty (1616 – 1911), when they also had their own priests and churchly schools.

Now, followers of Islam in China include a dozen other nationalities like the Uygurs, Kazaks and Tungsiangs, mostly living in Xinjiang Qinghai, Gansu and Ningxia.

Stone Tablet of the Koran in Islam

Introspection Tower

At Prayer

Xi'an Museum of Steles

Xi'an Museum of Steles stands east 0. 5km inside the South Gate of the City Wall of. As the most comprehensive collections stone works in Asia, the museum displays the main classics in morals, exemplary calligraphy and fine sculptures.

Throughout the Tang Dynasty (618 – 907) imperial examination system was the only way to enter an official career. The underdeveloped printing technology then made copying the sole means of reading and learning, which might result in careless slips of the pen. To end such practice of learning in view of the widespread influence of the 12 classics, say, The classic of Songs, The Classic of Rites, The Classic of History and The Classic of Changes, Emperor Li Ang of the Tang Dynasty gave the order in the year of 837 that the Imperial Academy get them all collated, inscribed on 114 separate pieces of stone (altogether 228 sides) and finally placed in the Imperial College as the standard for the nation. They were later known as The Kaicheng Stone Classics.

In 1090 of the Song Dynasty (960 – 1279), the Confucian Temple at the present site was constructed. Accordingly, *The Kaicheng*

Kaicheng Stone Classics

Stone Classics and *The Classic of Filial Piety* were both moved to the back of the temple. In the Qing Dynasty (1616 – 1911), another classic The Mencius, engraved on nine pieces of stone as and addition to *The Kaicheng Stone Classics*, brought the combined total to 13 classics. Best preserved among China's seven maior engraving activities and the heaviest works across the world, they deserve serious attention from Chinese and foreign scholars. After the Song Dynasty, the carved stone tablets were no longer transferred to some – where else and they were joined by more arrivals of either historic importance of calligraphic value. That contributed to the establishment of Forest of Steles in the present day. After China's liberation, the addition of stone sculptures and the inclusion of the Confucian Temple constitute the scale of size up – to – date.

Calligraphy by Wang Xizhi, Zhu Suiliang and Yan Zhengqing.

Mural Painting *Meeting Envoys*, from Tomb of Prince Zhang Huai

Upon entry into the museum, what meets the eye first is a square tablet pavilion with 2 floors. The pavilion has tablets inscribed the *Classic of Filial Piety*, whose wores were personally written and annotated in 745 by Emperor Li Longji (Xuanzong, reigned 712 – 756) of the Tang Dynasty, in as attempt to rule the nation by enhancing people's awareness of filial sentiments. Moreover, the tabets were placed on a mangnificent giant stone. So, *The Classic of Filial Piety* is otherwise known as The Classic of Filial Piety on Stone. The stone tablets magnificent appearance and unique in style, were carved in the fine offcial script of the Tang Dynasty.

Behind the tablet pavilion lies a U – shaped hall that devotes almost full floor space to the display of *The Kaicheng Stone Classics*. This exhibition hall, numbered the first, the largest in the museum.

No. 2 Exhibition Hall has inscribed tablets in the calligraphy of famous calligrphers from the Jin Dynasty (265 – 420) down to the Tang Dynasty. What merits special interest in *Tablet of Forward to the Holy Religion of Tang Dynasty*. Depite the forward composed by Emperor Li Shimin (Taizong, reigned 626 – 649) of the Tang Dynasty, the postscript produced by Emperor Li Zhi (Gaozong, reigned 649 – 683) of the Tang Dynasty and the two presentations made by Master Monk Xuanzhuang of the same

dynasty to express his thanks, the tablet was inscribed in the calligraphy of Master Calligrapher Wang Xizhi who lived in the middle of the Jin Dynasty. How was that? It turned out that Emperor Li Shimin envied the master's calligraphy so much so that Monk Huai Ten, Chief of Hongfu Buddhist Temloe, took painstaking efforts to buy the master's authentic characters at high price from common folks, Hence, the inscription was done to the delight of the emperor.

The Nestorian Tablet is an another precious relic that the world has ever known. It records how Nestorianism, a sect of Christianity in the Roman Empire, was introduced into China and became widely accepted. Meanwhile, it reflects extensive contacts and cultural exchanges that existed between the Tang Dynasty and the rest of the world 1, 300 years ago.

The exhibition halls from No. 3 to No. 7 center on collections of inscribed tablets in the authentic calligraphy of celebrated calligraphers belonging to different feudal dynasties. The rubbings over these tablets serve as models of calligraphy. For example, *Tablet of Genealogy of the Yan's Family* by Yan Zhenqing at the

venerable age of 72, *Epitphial Tablet to Da Da*, Master of the Law in the calligraphy of Liu Gongquan, *Tablet of Forward to the Holy Religion of Tongzhou Prefecture* by *Zhu Suiliang*, Epitaphial Tablet to Huangpu Dan by Ouyang Xung, Epitaphial Tablet to Dao Yin, Master of the Law by Ouyang Tong, inscriptions by grass script masters Zhang Xu and Huai Su, calligraphy works by Master Calligrapher Wang Xizhi, *Epitaphial Tablet to Cao Quan* in most distinguished official script of the Han Dynasy (206 B. C. – 220 A. D.), in addition to those inscribed in the calligraphy of other renowned calligraphers who lived in the Dynasties of Tang, Song, Yuan (1206 – 1368) Ming (1368 – 1644) and Qing.

As for the Exhibition Hall of Stone Sculptures , the inscription was written in Chinese by Chen Yi, China's late field marshal. In display in the hall are 70 odd pieces of scuplture works arranged in order of time. They fall into two categories: mausoleum scupltures and religion sculptures.

Stone sculpted beasts and statues of the Eastern Han Dynasty (25 – 220) were made by simple but forceful cuts. Buddha figures in the Tang Dynasty were modelled plump and close to nature.

Before Zhaoling Mausoleum of Emperor Li Shimin stand six engraved steeds. They look vigorous, graceful and true to life. The scuplture of a Buddha even wins the title of `Oriental Venus'. In a word, each of these fine sculptures fully reveals the superb craftsmanship and a highly artistic condensation acquired by the common people as well as by the artists of the ancient China.

Bronze Mirror, Tang Dynasty

Jade Head of a Buddha, Tang Dynasty

Tri – coloured Glazed Camel and Figurines, Tang Dynast

Xianyang Museum

Xianyang Museum lies in the proper of Xianyang City, 25km west of Xi'an. It was completed in 1962 with expansion of the Confucian Temple.

Historically, Xianyang served as the seat of capital when China became unified under the rule of the Qin Dynasty (221 - 206 B. C.) Neverthrless, The city remains to be the communications hub linking China's expansive northwest nowadays.

The Northern Tableland of Xianyang is where the Western Han Dynasty (206 B. C - 25

A. D.), had five emperors buried. The sites of five imperial mausoleums make the land known as Wuling Hillock (meaning Tableland of Five Mausoleums), Therefore, the relics there are richly endowed in cultural sense, whether aboveground or underground.

The museum houses over 12, 000 pieces of cultural relics dating back to such dynasties as Zhou (11th century – 771 B. C.), Qin (221 – 206 B. C.), Han (206 B. C. – 220 A . D) and Tang (618 – 907) . A mong the well – known relics are a tripod called *Xia Guan Zhong* made at Anyi County and a vessel called *Fu Wen Bei* made at Xiuwu County. They provide important source materials and proofs in the study of the Qin Dynasty from the time when Shang Yang (390 – 338B. C.) pushed forward reforms to the time when the nation became unified.

The museum comprises 7 separate exhibition rooms, containing Xianyang historical relics of Qin Dynasty (3 rooms), relics from inperial mausoleums of Western Han Dynasty (one room), over 3, 000 Western Han colour – painted pottery warriors and horses unerathed at Yangjiawan Village (2 rooms) and another room is reserved in case of need.

The exhibits that stand out most are jade carvings of the Western han Dynasty. They look smooth and transparent all over with ingenious and delicate impressions. Large numbers of the relics have had successul shows in USA, Japan, Italy and Singapore.

Pottery Horse Rider, Han Dynasty

Brick with Dragon Designs, Han Dynasty

Bell Tower

Bell Tower stands in the center of Xi'an and at the intersection of the four straight roads running east, west, north and south, at the end of each of which is a gate tower that stands opposite to the Tower at a distance.

The square tower of 36m in height over a floor space of 1, 377m² was constructed on an eight – metre – high rostrum of blue brick, with through gateways from north to south and from west to east.

The tower was first built on Guangji Street, 0. 5km west of Drum Tower, in 1384 of the Ming Dynasty （1368 – 1644）. It was moved to the present site in 1582. The tower of wood – tenoned structure without a nail has two floors, with a winding corridor on the upper floor. It has carved beams and painted rafters, with application of gole foil to the both. It is roofed by green glazed tiles, with projecting eaves underneath in double layers turning up a little at the edges. The tip extends to 5m high, coated in gold.

Bell Tower used to tell the time daily. The sound of striking reached far and wide.

Drum Tower

Drum Tower stands on the West Street in the heart of Xi' an and 400m west of Bell Tower.

Drum Tower was constructed in 1380 of the Ming Dynasty (1368 – 1644). It is a structure of 33m high, with projecting eaves turning up a little at the edges.

The tower used to have a huge drum placed on the upper floor. The drum was used to tell the time. Down the tower traffic vehicles go northsouth and back through the gateway.

Drum Tower is of unusually solid architecture. It has withstood a dozen of quakes without single cranny for 500 years.

Shaanxi History Museum

Shaanxi History Museum is located south of Xi'an 4km off the city proper, with the Big Wild Goose Pagoda. It used to hold a show place in Beilin Museum of Steles. However, the place seemed pitiably small to afford the full display huge quantities of relics. which was brought to completion in 1991 under the personal concern of China's late premier Zhou Enlai and opened to the public in the same year.

With a floor space of 65, 000m², the museum was constructed over an area of 60, 000m²

to imitate the architectural style of the Tang Dynasty (618 – 907). It ranks as the nation's second largest in magnitude, next to Palace Museum.

Shaanxi History Museum administers modern management throughout. Self – designed facilities were installed to protect effctively against occurence of fire and theft for the safety of the stored relics. Closed – circuit TV systems keep close watch all the time. Infrared detectors monitor every inch of land in the halls

Bronze Tripod, Western
Zhou Dynasty

Bronze Arch Chime, Western Zhou Dynasty

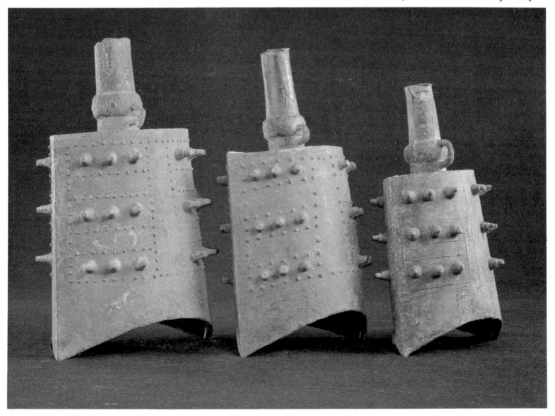

Maids of Honour Holding Round Fans,
from Tomb of Prince Zhang Huai

of the museum. In case something abnormal
crops up, videocopiers will truly get scenes
recorded without delay.

The museum collects most of the mural
paintings found in tombs of the Tang Dynasty.
To better preserve the treasures storage chambers were so designed that they were built on
rails and enclosed on all sides, with a constant
temperature and moisture void of ultraviolet
rays. The mural paintings are hung in chambers
that run on rails. Press down the button and the
chambers will go out and back gently. Such
design is indeed ingenious.

The museum keeps varieties of unearthed
relics that amount to 370,000 pieces as many.
Quite a few are top – notch treasures of the
national grade. For example, a solid bronze
tripod of solid build called *Wai Shu Ding* and a
four legged bronze wine vessel of unique shape
are among the most influential in the relic fan
circles.

Pottery figures as important ancient relics

Painted Pottery Figurine, Tang Dynasty

Mural Painting *In Hot Pursuit of Game*, from Tomb of Prince Zhang Huai

Mural Painting *Hunting Procession*, from Tomb of Prince Zhang Huai

Bronze Chime Bell, Westem Zhou Dynasty

Bird – Patterned Bronze Ware, Westem Zhou Dynasty

Painted Pottery Horse and Rider, Tang Dynasty

left over by history are found time and again across the country. However, it is a rare case that the unearthed figures in Shaanxi date far back from the Spring and Autumn Period (770 – 476 B. C.) down to the Dynasties of Ming (1368 – 1644) and Qing (1616 – 1911). They not only abound in number, but vary with dynasties in shape – moulding and craftsman-ship.

The museum displays full mural paintings in a special way from tombs of the Tang Dynasty in 1952. Now, such paintings that have been taken off total to 1, 000m², when put together. Apart from high value of artistic appreciation, they serve as necessary data in the study of so-cial intercoures, cultural life and customary

77

A mural painting in the tomb of crowned prince YIDE

clothing of the Tang Dynasty, as is seen in Foreign Envoys Polo Game on Horseback and Maids of Honour, to name a few.

The museum stores the most quantities of gold and silver wares of the nation. It is estimated that the museum has over 900 such wares. The most distinguished are those that were unearthed at Heijia Village of Xi' an in 1970. Many are of marvellous design and ingenious creation. For instance, agate cup shaped like an ox head whose mouth is inlaid with gold and goldgilt silver pot with two

punched horese attached.

The museum, when inaugurated, added 2, 200 more pieces of unearthed relics on display. For instance, *gold – gilt fumigator* on a bronze supporter with joints from Maoling Mausoleum and goose – patterned bronze lamp from Shenmu County.

The museum, featured with magnificent architecture, first – rate equipment and abundant varieties of relics, is putting on fresh looks to attract more Chinese and foreign visitors.

Bird's – Eye View of Shuilu Buddhist Temple

Shuilu Buddhist Temple

Shuilu Buddhist Temple is situated 10km east of Lantian Township and 40km east of Xi'an. As is recorded in the *Annals of Lantian County*, the temple, built in 3rd century, was a part of Wunzhen Buddhist Temple and attracted Buddhist worshippers in their thousands. The temple was surrounded by water on three sides with another side nearby green hills, so the name was later changed to Shuilu Buddhist Temple (meaning a temple with water and land around).

The most impressive is the main hall of the temple. Except for the gates, the other three walls of the hall bear 3, 700 odd coloured sculptures. The scuptures on the northern and southern walls tell an interesting story of

Sakyamuni, founder of Buddhism, in lifelike and imaginative descriptions of waters, hills, trees, pavilions, birds and animals. They disclose how Buddhism mingled with the native culture 1,000 years after is was introduced into China . Moreover, the postures of 500 sculpted Buddhist arhats are meant to say that only by practising asceticism can man free himself from the endless sea of human bitterhess to finally enter Heaven.

On the western wall are scenes that show the sculpted worshippers listening humbly to Sakyamuni explaning the sutra.

Groups of the coloured scupltures express unity of Confucianism, Taoism and Buddhism as well as their independence of one another, that is, the philosophical thinking represented by Confucius, Lao Zi and Sakyamuni repectively not opposing but equally important in China.

Legend has it that the coloured sculptures were made by Yang Huizhi, a master sculptor of the Tang Dynasty (618 – 907). Whether true of not, the superb craftsmanship and rich imagination together with ingenious approach speak loudly of the fact that all would have been impossible if it were done by an average man.

Three Buddhas

Grand Buddha, Tang Dynasty

Temple of Grand Buddha

The Temple of Grand Buddha stands 10km west of Binxian County and 190km west of Xi'an. It was built in 629 at the order of Emperor Li Shimin (Taizong, reigned 626 – 649) in the hope that it would bestow happiness and long life upon his mother. An extra huge statue of Buddha was engraved into the hill, hence the name of the temple.

Legend goes that four cowboys once went up the hill to herd cattle. They heard a voice asking them whether is was time to build a temple on the hill. No sooner had the affirmative answer been made casually by one cowboy than the hill split with an explosive crash and the Buddha was seen sitting in the crack. The legend led to the construction of the temple.

The Temple of Grand Buddha that stands 30m high was constructed along the hill. It is comprised of Rock Cave of Grand Buddha, Grottos of Buddhism Arhats and Grottos of Thousand Buddhas.

Rock Cave of Grand Buddha houses 3 Buddhas, the Largest among which is the 24 – meter – high statue of colour fully decorated Sakyamuni sitting unruffled against the hill on the seat of lotus. The Buddha has hair combed in spiral style, big mouth on broad face, ears drooping to the shoulder, open breast and two silk stripes tied under the waist. Moreover, widespreda rays of buddhism light were engraved in the hill behind the Buddha, above whose top the cave bears engravings of 19 flying – Apsaras of various postures in basrelief. To either side of the Buddha stand Buddhism Kuanyin and Buddhism Dashizhi, each 5m in height. In the interior walls of the cave were carved 600 expressive stone statues of Buddhas.

From there up are Grottos of Buddhism Arhats, in which there are stone sculptures of arhats and Buddhas, together with 60 pieces of bas – relief works that tell Buddha's episodes.

Grottos of Thousand Buddhas, situated 100m east of Rock Cave of Grand Buddha, have almost the same number of Buddhas as in Grottos of Buddhism Arhats, bas – relief works in greater number.

The magnificent magnitued of the grottos and the artistic engravings express the momentum in simplicity that existed early in the Tang Dynasty (618 – 907). Now, they are listed as important relics under the special protection of the state.

Temple of Grand Buddha

Wuzhang Hillock

Wuzhang Hillock Lies 20km south of Qishan County and 130km west of Xi'an. It stands 130m high, with Qinling Mountain Range to the south and Weihe River to the north.

Topographic separation of Wuzhang Hillock from Hanzhong in southern Shaanxi because of Qinling Mountains was linked in the ancient times by a plank roadway wedged into the mountain cliffs. In the Period of Three Kingdoms (221 – 263), Zhuge Liang (181 – 234), Chancellor of the Shu Kingdom (211 – 263), commanded his army up north across the narrow passage six times to station the troops at the other side of the mountains. The military operations aimed to annihilate the Kingdoms of Wei (220 – 265) and Wu (222 – 280) and to finally realize his lifelong wish of seeing a unified China. He led his army pitted against troops of the Wei Kingdom under the command of Sima Yi. During the battles, Zhuge Loang plotted to lure troops of the Wei Kingdom in deep. When burning blocked their retreat and the troops were about to be practically wiped out, a sudden downpour saved them out of imminent annihilation. The well – planned plot

Zhuge Liang

went up like a bubble, as is explained in the proverb: Man proposes, God disposes.

Zhuge Liang died in the army tent pitched at Wuzhang Hillock as a result of intense work on military affairs. When Sima Yi heard of the news, troops of the Shu Kingdom had already withdrawn safely to Hanzhong under camouflage. The arrangements of this withdrawal was made by Zhuge Liang, whose military talent was highly admired by Sima Yi.

Wu Hou Temple of Zhuge Liang was built in 13th century and repairs were done in the Dynasties of Ming (1368 – 1644) and Qing (1616 – 1911). Mural paintings in the temple are telling romance of the three kingdoms. In there too, 40 pieces of limestone are put up that bear the admonishment of Zhuge Liang before his two battle expeditions in smooth calligralhy of Yue Fei, a distinguished army officer of the Song Dynasty (960 – 1270).

Wu Hou Temple at Wuzhang Hillock is one among the same major sort in China. The other two are in Chengdu of Sichuan Province and at Wolong Ridge of Hubei Province.

Memorial Temple to Sima Qian

Memorial Temple to Sima Qian

The Memorial Temple to Sima Qian and his tomb are positioned at Zhichuan Township where he was borh. The township is seated 10km south of Hancheng City but 200km northeast of Xi'an.

Sima Qian was a historian, a man of letters as well as a thinker that lived in the Western Han Dynasty (206 B. C. – 25 A. D.) Noted for meticulous studies, he went across the whole country to do textual research on the cause of every historic event and the site where it took place. With reference to reliable and substantial data, he began to work on matters of great account in China's history.

This was the time when the dynasty was at war with the Huns, to whom Li Ling, an officer of the dynasty, Surrendered. Sima Qian argued in favour of the officer. For that reason he was wrongly treated and castrated. In spite of immense mental and physical pains, he never gave up his determination to finish writing. He worked his heart out and successfully produced a huge book that comprised 130 pieces of details in 520, 000 characters. The book Recores of the Historian won him immortal fame and left an influential mark in history.

The memorial temple and tomb were constructed in Oline with the terain of the mountain. Seen from below, the structure looks like a fortress built on four plots of teraced land at separate heights. The terraced plot at the top is the location of the temple and the tomb.

The temple has the chamber for placement of sacrificial offerings in the front and sleeping quarters in the rear, where the statue of Sima Qian is seen sitting upright in a niche, flanked by 64 stone tablets that recorded his indelible contributions.

Behind the sleeping quarters in the tomb. It takes the shape of a cylinder laid with green bricks, whose surface was carved with the Eight Trigrams and other designs.

Away from the tomb is a village inhabited mostly by people bearing the surnames of Feng and Tong. They all say that they are descen-

dants of the Sima Family. The matter turns out that during the Western Han Dynasty members of the Sima Family, for fear of involvement, split the double – character family name into two single – character surnames, to the either of which strokes were added on the left side to form the new characters of Feng and Tong. The aim of so doing was to continue the genealogical tree of the Sima Family even if disaster of a family massacre involving the case of Sima Qian might befall by imperial order. Even now, the two families don't have marriage bonds but retain the custom of offering sacrifices to their common ancestor Sima Qian.

Tomb of Sima Qian

Northem Foot of Yaowang Mountain

Yaowang Mountain

Yaowang Mountain lies 1.5km east of Yaoxian County and 120km north of Xi' an. It used to be the holy place of both buddhism and taoism from the Tang Dynasty (618 – 907) through the Five Dynasties (907 – 960).

Sun Simiao, a medical specialist of the Tang Dynasty, studied medicine tirelessly throughout life. Based on the attainments by his predecessors and his own medical practice, he wrote indelible works lide Thousand Presripions and Continuation to Thousand Prescriptions.

They are the treasures in the pharmacognosy of the Chinese medicine. Moreover, as an ethical doctor, he practised medicine in out – of – the – way cillages where medical treatment was mostly needed. All that earned him a very high reputation of master doctor both in the medical circles and among the common people. After his death , talbets were erected and a temple built to commemorate his devoted contribution to medicine and his noble medical ethics. And the mountain where he lived in seclusion late in

his lifetime is now known as Yaowang Mountain (meaning master doctor – lived mountain).

The statue of Sun Simiao and the temple built in his memory stand on top of the mountain. There are also the cave where Wun Simiao lived, the pools where medicinal herbs were washed, the cypresses planted by Sun Simiao, the passage along which Emperor Li Simiao, ancient architectures dating back to the Jin Dynasty (1115 – 1234) and the Yuan Dynasty (1206 – 1368) and mural paintings of the latter dynasty.

Sun Simiao

Now, the mountain is on the list of important relics under the protection of the state.

Mt. Yaowang has no lack of stone sculptures that were carved into cliffs, among which are those of the Sui (581 – 618) and Tang Dynasties. The artistic scuptures of superb approach are now placed under the special protection of the state. Apart from that, the stone sculptures with characters carved in the reign of Emperor Yuan Xu (516 – 528) of the Northern Wei Dynasty (386 – 534) are thought of as treasures. of the nation. And the characters themselves are recommended as calligraphy models of the time. Calligraphy fans from Japan even go there to see and leam.

Buddha

Former Site of Hongmen Feast

Former Site of Hongmen Feast

The former site of Hongmen Feast lies at Hongmenpu Village, 35km east of Xi'an.

Towards the late stage of the Qin Dynasty (221 – 206 B. C.), Xiang Yu and Liu Bang, heads of the peasant uprising army, took two different routes, along which they led their army to attack Xianyang, capital of the Qin Dynasty. They both agreed that who first took hold of the capital should be the ruler. Xiang Yu fought Hard all the way through, whereas Liu Bang met less fierce resistance because he adopted a policy of appeasing the captive. So, the army led by Liu Bang reached the capital early and captured Emperor Zi Ying (grandson of Qin Shi Hung). However, Liu Bang daren't station his army in Xianyang for fear of Xiang Yu, a man of power. Recognizing the threat from the opponent , Fan Zeng, counsellor to Xiang Tu planned a scheme to kill Liu Bang on the pretext of inciting him to a feast at Hongmen. That is the origin of the Chinses proverb; Xiang Zhuang performed the sword dance as a cover his attempt on Liu Bang's life.

The formere site of Hongmen Feast was laid of blue brick. There in the army tent are sculptures depicting such scenes as Xiang Zhuang (officer under Xiang Yu) performing the sword dance, Fan Kuai (officer under Liu Bang) breaking into the thent, Liu Nang leaving the feast and Fan Zeng heaving long sighs.

Mt. Huashan

Mt. Huashan lies in Huayin County and 120km east of Xi' an. It is 2, 200m above sea level. Seen from a distance, it resembles the shape of lotus in blossom.

Out of the five famous mountains * in China, Mt. Huashan is the extraordinarily perilous but peculiar, hence the name of No. 1 precipitous mount under Heaven.

Most travellers used to turn back before the steep Thousand – Foot – High Precipice and a huge rock lying there is thus known as Back Rock. From there up are breath – taking cliffs of Hundred – Foot – High Gorge and Lao Jun Gully (Lao Jun, patriarch of Taoism), but Blue Dragon Ridge bears the threatening momentum. A story tells that Han Yu of the Tang Dynasty (618 – 907) got so frightened on ridge that the great poet dropped his book to cry for help. Father upwards are Chess Pavilion, Cliffside Roadway and Sparrow Hawk Cliff that look all the more terrifying.

Many legends spread of Mt. Huashan, e. g., Save Mother to Split the Mountain and Emperor Zhao Kuangyin (Taizu, reigned 960 – 976) Priced Mt. Huashan for Loss of Chess Game.

Chess Pavilion

West Peak of Mt. Huashan

The familiar saying has been One Road Leading Up to Mt. Huashan. Now, another road has been built under the North Peak for the convenience to climb the top. Moreover, a cableway has been installed that even the disabled can go up to the North Peak by cable car.

* Five famous mountains: Mt. Taishan in Shandong, Mt Huashan in Shaanxi, Mt. Heng – shan in Hunan Mt. Hengshan (same pronunciation but different name) in Shanxi and Mt. Sonshan in Henan.

Cliffside Roadway

Remains of Yaozhou Kilns

The remains of Yaozhou Kilns lie at Huangpu Township of Tongchuan City, 90km north of Xi'an.

The location of Yaozhou kilns in on the loess Plateau of clay soil. Production of porcelain wares there began in the Sui (581 – 618) and Tang (618 – 907) Dynasties, but climaxed in the Song Dynasty (960 – 1279). And Huangpu Township was then known as a place of kilns in clusters. However, wuch pomp no longer existed after the Dynasties of Yuan (1206 – 1368) and Ming (1368 – 1644).

In 1984, excavation of the township by the Shaanxi Provincial Archaeological Institute led to a fruitful discovery of over 40 former kiln sites and over 50 fire – pits. The unearthed relics include tools, porcelain pieces and ornamental objects. Those of the Tang Dynasty are black or ornamental procelain, but those of the Song Dynasty are yellow, pale blue and celadon porcelain, with the latter in the most quantity. The decorative desings are largely of lotus, apart form peony, phoenix, crane, fish and duck. The usual approach was to carve

Glazed Bottom – Infused Pot

designs in bas – relief or in smooth lineage.

A protective hall was constructed at the former site of kilns in 1988. It stands along the Xi' an – Tongchuan Highway. To the west is Yaozhou Kilns Museum that faces opposite to the hall. In the museum rich varieties of unearthed porcelain are on display. Moreover, visitors watch the entire process in porcelain production and can even take a try with their own hands.

Authors: Luo Xiaofei   Yao Xuefeng
Translators: Qin Yuyin (1 – 24)
                Wei Lingcha (25 – 59)
                Lu Zuben (60 – 96)
Editors: Shi Guolin Li Dan
Photographers: Guo Youmin Wang Lei
Designer: Wang Lei
Illustrator: Wang Haijing

作　　者:姚雪峰　罗笑菲
翻　　译:秦余荫(1 – 24)
　　　　魏令查(25 – 59)
　　　　陆祖本(60 – 96)
编　　辑:史国霖　李　丹　张春峰
摄　　影:郭佑民　王　磊
设　　计:王　磊
插图作者:王海静

XI' AN: Places of
Historical Interest
– Memories of Chang' an –

Published by: Xi' an World Publishing Corporation
                 17 South Street
                 Xi' an, China
Distributed by: XI' AN BRANCH OF CHINA NATIONAL PUBLICATIONS
                 IMPORY AND EXPORY CORPORATION
                 No. 93 Nan Da Jie
                 Xi' an China
Edition: First Edition

ISBN: 7 – 5062 – 3287 – 1/Z · 47   XB0006000